D1119877

Positively for Kids®
Kirkland Avenue Office Park
8II Kirkland Avenue, Suite 200
Kirkland, WA 98033
www.positivelyforkids.com

© 2004 by Positively For Kids, Inc.
All rights reserved.
No part of this book may be reproduced or utilized in any form or by means electronic or
mechanical including photocopying, recording or by any information storage and retrieval system,
without permission of the copyright holders.
All Internet sites were available and accurate when sent to press.

Bird, Sue, I980-
Sue Bird—Be Yourself/ by Sue Bird with Greg Brown.
48-p.: ill. (mostly col.), ports.; 26 cm (Positively for Kids)
Summary: Recounts the life of Sue Bird, former UConn basketball player and point guard for the
Seattle Storm, and her belief that to succeed in sports as well as in life, one must be true to oneself.
Audience: Grades 4-8

ISBN 0-9634650-5-8

I. Bird, Sue, I980-. Juvenile literature. 2. Women basketball players—United States—Biography—
Juvenile literature. [I. Bird, Sue, I980-. 2. Women basketball players—Biography.] I. Brown, Greg,
1957-. II. Title.

796.323/092—dc2I[B]

Library of Congress Control Number:
2004094285

Photo Credits:
All photos courtesy of Sue Bird and family except the following:
John Froschauer/AP/Wide World: 38 bottom right. Jeffrey Phelps/AP/Wide World: 33 right. Gene
J. Puskar/AP/Wide World: 3I. Corbis: 46 right. Basketball Hall of Fame: 46 left. Getty Images: 46
middle. Ray Amati/NBAE/Getty Images: 40 right. Bill Baptist/NBAE/Getty Images: 43 right. Nathaniel
S. Butler/NBAE/Getty Images: 38 middle left; 38 bottom left. Chris Covatta/NBAE/Getty Images:
45. Jesse D. Garrabrant/NBAE/Getty Images: 38 top right. Barry Gossage/NBAE/Getty Images:
35. Ron Hopkins/NBAE/Getty Images: 40 left. Fernando Medina/NBAE/Getty Images: 6. Jennifer
Pottheiser/NBAE/Getty Images: 5; 32 left. Jeff Reinking/NBAE/Getty Images: Cover; 38 top left; 42;
43 left. Shem Roose/NBAE/Getty Images: 36; 37. Michael Ash "Copyright, 1997, Newsday. Reprinted
with permission.": 25 left. Nike: 40 middle. UConn Athletic Communications: 26; 28 left; 28 middle;
28 right; 29 left; 29 right; 30 left; 30 middle; 30 right; 32 right; 33 top left; 33 bottom left.

Special Thanks:
Positively For Kids would like to thank the people and organizations that helped make this book
possible: Sue Bird; her family and friends; Dan Levy of Octagon; and the Seattle Storm.

Book Design:
Methodologie Inc., Seattle

Printed in Canada

SUE
BIRD

BE
YOURSELF

BY SUE BIRD
WITH GREG BROWN

A POSITIVELY FOR KIDS BOOK

Hi! I'm Sue Bird.

I've loved playing sports my whole life. I've loved sports for the same reasons boys love sports. I love the challenge, the competition, the action, the drama, the athletic skill, the teamwork, and the friendships.

I never had childhood dreams of playing in the Women's National Basketball Association. That's because the WNBA didn't exist when I was young. The first WNBA season was in 1997, my junior year in high school. I did dream about playing in the Olympics.

After playing in two high school state basketball championships and two NCAA national basketball championships, I was the No. 1 pick in the WNBA draft in 2002.

Now I am living a dream by playing basketball and getting paid to do what I love. In my professional career I've been an All-Star, been in the playoffs, and know what it's like to miss the playoffs.

YEAR **2003**

YEAR **1988**

On my way to the WNBA, I dealt with teasing in school for being a tomboy.

I know what it's like to be the only girl on an all-boys team.

I know the thrill of being a leader and I know the pain of watching from the sidelines thanks to a season-ending injury. I know a little bit about fame and what it's like to be embarrassed on a national scale.

Sports is a great teacher and has taught me much about life—and most importantly about myself. Sports brings out the truth—true emotions, true skills, and true motivation. To be successful you can't be someone you're not. You can't fake it on the field of play or off it, at least not for very long. You have to be yourself.

I've written this book to share with you my true life story. These pages will give you glimpses of me and maybe things inside yourself. Some are funny, some are strange, a few are sad. But they are all true. My hope is they will give you the courage to be your best self.

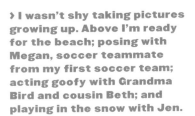

> I wasn't shy taking pictures growing up. Above I'm ready for the beach; posing with Megan, soccer teammate from my first soccer team; acting goofy with Grandma Bird and cousin Beth; and playing in the snow with Jen.

> Jen and I are ready to go for Halloween, but I don't remember what I was supposed to be in a black hat and cape.

> Jen and I are all smiles in this formal picture.

I got hooked on sports thanks to my only sister, Jen. She is five years older and she always played sports.

I went to all her games. My father, Herschel, a doctor, enjoyed sports. My mom, Nancy, a nurse, would rather read a good book than watch sports, unless, of course, her daughters were playing. Then she'd only read during timeouts and halftime of our youth games.

My parents gave Jen and me a perfectly good suburban upbringing in Syosset, New York, which is on Long Island, 25 miles east of New York City. They supported us in all our activities and interests. I really had it pretty good. For Jen, on the other hand, life wasn't all that easy because of me.

We had our sisterly squabbles over everything. I wanted what Jen had. She was my measuring stick.

FUN FACT >>> SUE WAS BORN 10/16/1980. HER BIRTH CERTIFICATE READS: SUZANNE BRIGIT BIRD.

I MADE IT MY JOB TO BUG HER. I WOULDN'T LEAVE HER ALONE, ESPECIALLY WHEN SHE GOT OLDER AND HAD BOYFRIENDS AT OUR HOUSE.

I'd play video games with her boyfriends. As I matured, my relationship with Jen got easier.

She's been a great sister to put up with me. Even though I made a living being the annoying little sister, by the time I got to high school she forgave me. From then on she was always there for me. Whether I was upset about my parents or needed help with my math homework, from the smallest questions to the biggest problems, I could turn to her. It was great having an older sister! Now I get calls from her to make her CDs all the time, legally, of course. She's probably thinking it's great to have a little sister these days.

But not when I first beat her in basketball. I was 9, she was 14. We were at the nearby basketball court. After I won, she "accidentally" tripped me. I landed face-first on the concrete and chipped my right front tooth. We searched the court on our hands and knees but couldn't find the bottom half of the tooth. The dentist did the best he could to match my tooth color. But even today, if you see me close up you'll notice where it was chipped. Keep that a secret though ☺.

> I'm standing in our driveway with a neighbor's house in the background.

I have a small scar above my left eye. It happened near our summer home in Saratoga, New York. I hit my head on a car door and needed stitches. My parents took me to a hospital but the emergency room was crowded. With Dad being a doctor, he didn't want to wait—he cleaned it and put on a butterfly Band-Aid. This scar is my favorite because it makes me look tough. (Ha ha, that's partly a joke.) The real reason I like scars is because I think they give a person some character, especially on the face. They show that nobody is perfect. I'm also proud of the one on my knee from my ACL surgery. It's a reminder I made it through tough times.

THE
WOODS

ONTARIO
er Bay

Moosonee

Cochrane

Timmins
Rouyn

Sault Ste
Marie
Sudbury

Ottawa

QUEBEC

MISTASSINI

ST LAWRENCE

Quebec

Rimou

Charlotte

Fredericton NB

Montreal MAINE

L SUPERIOR
perior

Green
S Bay

Madison

ukee

cago

M I C H I G A N

MICH

HURON

Lansing

London

Detroit

Toledo

Windsor

L ERIE

Toronto

L ONT

Roch
ester

Buffalo

PA

Pittsburgh

VT

NY

Montpelier

NH

Concord

Albany

Boston

MASS

Halt

CONN

Providence

New York

Gary

Cleveland

OHIO

Columbus

IND

ll

eld

Indianapolis

Cincinnati

Harrisburg

MD

Trenton

N

Phi

hia

DE

Louis

Louisville

HIO

KY

Frank-
fort

TENN

emphis

Nashville

W VA

Charleston

Baltimore

Dover

Washington

Richmond

VA.

Philadelphia

Syosset, Long Island
New York

Chattanooga

APPALACHIAN MTS

NC

Raleigh

ALA

ham

GA

SC

Columbia

C Hatteras

Atlanta

nery

Augusta

Charleston

obile

Columbus

Savannah

attahassee

Jacksonville

eans

t Petersbur

> My first grade class picture with my pet monster, which didn't have a name other than "Pet Monster."

> I show my love of music with my fake electric guitar.

You could say I was hardwired to be competitive. We played board and card games as a family growing up. Candy Land and Chutes and Ladders were early favorites. I must admit I was a cheater. Because I was the youngest, they let me get away with it. I'd peek at cards when someone stepped away from the table momentarily. I'd mark cards. I'd throw a fit if I lost. I was such a sore loser.

I did play with Barbies. I had a Barbie house and everything. I didn't see toys as a girl thing or boy thing. I just wanted to try new things. In first grade I had a pet monster. I took it to school every day. He even made it in my first grade class picture. I enjoyed building toy robots when I was 10. I had a pink tent over my bed, shaped like a house. That became my fortress for months in third grade. Even though I hate pink, I spent a lot of time in my tent, until my dog, Mindy, spent so much time in there with me that my room smelled like puppy dog tails. My mom wasn't too happy about that.

I'd wear dresses, occasionally. But I was most comfortable in sports clothes such as sweats. I have naturally curly hair. I always longed for different hair. It took 30 minutes every day to fix my hair just the way I like it—straight with no curls unless I'm playing sports, in which case I always wear it in a ponytail.

FUN FACT >>> ONE DAY WHILE THROWING ROCKS IN FRONT OF HER HOUSE, SUE ACCIDENTALLY SHATTERED A WINDOW OF HER MOM'S CAR.

> Brad and I at our first sporting event together.

> Playing at the beach with two friends from my all-boys soccer team.

> I'm in deep conversation in my tie-dye jeans.

I LOVED DOING EVERYTHING THE BOYS IN MY NEIGHBORHOOD LIKED TO DO—RIDE BIKES, PLAY WHATEVER SPORT WAS IN SEASON AT THE NEARBY PARK, OR CLIMB TREES. I WAS A TOMBOY.

In fact my best friend in the world, Brad Barnett, thought I was a boy at first. Our families knew each other because Jen played sports with his older sister. So I met Brad when we were toddlers. We played together at our sisters' games and our families became friends. I had pretty short hair and could do everything he could athletically. One day I wore a dress and freaked him out. We'd been playing together for some time and all along he thought I was a boy. He refused to play with me for a couple of months. He came around though. He's like a brother to me now and we talk about everything.

I'D LIKE TO SAY I WAS FEARLESS AND NEVER CRIED, BUT THAT'S NOT TRUE. I CRIED WHEN I GOT MY EARS PIERCED AT AGE 6. THE POP OF A PIERCING GUN CAN BE TERRIFYING.

Waterskiing grew into one of my biggest fears. We had a ski boat and would take it out on Saratoga Lake in the summer. My sister, Jen, of course, could ski by the time I was old enough to try. So the summer I turned 5 it was my time to learn. Dad got in the water and helped me line up and keep my skis steady. Mom drove and Jen was the spotter. I got up fine the first time and was singing to myself "La-la-la-la" because I was so relaxed skiing. It seemed easy. Then I fell and forgot to let go of the rope. I remember the blasting rush of water against my face as I "submarined" through the water. Finally I heard "Let go!" and I did.

After checking to see if I was OK, Mom asked if I wanted to try again. "Sure," I said. Dad got me ready again. Just before she started, Mom said, "Don't forget to let go if you fall."

As soon as I heard that I wanted back in the boat. I didn't ski again for five years. I don't remember if falling or forgetting to let go scared me the most but I do remember feeling the water rushing into my face and I didn't like that at all.

> My seventh-grade school soccer team.

Another fear I had arose that fall at my very first soccer game for 5-year-olds. Mom drove me to my first game, and I refused to get out of the car.

"I can't go, I can't go," I pleaded. "I know I'm going to use my hands."

I knew only goalies could use their hands in soccer, but I was worried I would forget and pick up the soccer ball with my hands. Mom gave me reassurance and encouragement. I did finally get out of the car. Turns out I had a great game, scoring lots of goals.

Soccer became my second-favorite sport. I might have received a college scholarship for soccer if I had stuck with it.

I played on many great soccer teams and still stay in touch with former soccer teammates. We did a lot of traveling and our teams won our state tournament five times and attended two national tournaments.

> I endured braces two years—sixth and seventh grades—and cut my lips and inside my mouth a million times playing sports even though I put on protective wax.

> Three soccer teammates and I pose on the beach.

> My seventh grade CYO basketball team, coached by my sister.

As I advanced in soccer it got to the point where I was asked to play on an all-boys team when I was 11 years old. There were no girls teams in Syosset for that age, so I had no other choice.

IT WAS TOUGH AT FIRST. I KNEW HALF THE GUYS ON THE TEAM FROM MY SCHOOL, BUT THE OTHER HALF WENT TO A DIFFERENT SCHOOL. AT FIRST THEY DIDN'T ACCEPT ME.

The coach needed to call a team meeting to talk about it—that was embarrassing!

After they saw I could play the game, the problems went away. They called me "Tail," in honor of my ponytail. Two seasons later, I found a girls team from nearby Huntington and switched back to playing against girls.

A few years later, we were losing 0-1 with time running out in a state semifinal game. Just when we thought time ran out, a penalty was called. The referee said the game was over after the kick. Our coach picked me to shoot. A goal would send the match into overtime, a miss would send us home. I kicked it and the goalie made the stop. I immediately burst into tears. I felt I let down the whole team. This experience was horrible for me and one I'll never forget. I never wanted to feel like that again. It was my first taste of failure and I wouldn't have that taste again until my second season with the Storm.

I got teased some at elementary school, too, because I was such a jock and because I was a late bloomer. I was one of the last in my age group to develop curves, finally in the ninth grade. My sister, however, was an early bloomer, which gave me hope.

Nobody enjoys being teased. I didn't like it. It bothered me, but what I found was the guys who teased me the most soon wanted to ask me out. So if they teased me, I figured, they must like me. I got through it, and it didn't last long. Plus, I was secure with myself. I figured if those people didn't like the real me, then it was no big loss.

I truly did enjoy playing many sports. At various ages, I tried gymnastics, swimming, lacrosse, volleyball, golf, and track and field. Trying new sports came easy to me. I ran fast and showed good hand-eye coordination. If I had to pick a worst sports activity when I was young, I'd have to say miniature putt-putt golf. I didn't have the patience for it. I'd hit the ball three or four times as it rolled.

I didn't have much desire to sit still in elementary school and study. School really didn't interest me. Jen, on the other hand, is brilliant and always did extremely well in school. She graduated from Yale Law School and is an attorney.

So in my early years of elementary school Mom thought something was wrong with me. She thought I had a learning disability. It's true—I am more of a visual and auditory learner. If I hear something, it tends to stick more than when I read it. I wasn't a strong reader in elementary school. I didn't have an interest in reading, except one magazine. I read *Sports Illustrated For Kids* every month from cover to cover.

› Jen and I at the bottom of a slide stop for a picture.

› My friend Keira and I played on a fifth grade basketball team while in second grade so our local newspaper took our picture. My first press clip!

NOW, HOWEVER, I READ ALL THE TIME. WHEN I'M FLYING OR WAITING IN AIRPORTS, I'M ALWAYS READING.

I do have an uncanny memory. I can hear songs just one time and know them by heart. Or I can watch a movie and quote almost every line in the movie. I also have a great sense of direction. I can see maps in my head. One night Mom and I were driving through New York. I fell asleep, and Mom took a wrong turn into a rough part of Brooklyn. We called Dad and I got on the phone. Once he told us where we were from the cross streets, I quickly figured out how to get back to the freeway.

But in early elementary school I just wasn't trying. I wasn't that interested in school. I remember getting motivated when I was moved to a lower class. I thought, "They must think I'm dumb."

So I started working at school like I worked at sports. Within two weeks I was back in the upper class.

I worked hard for good grades, which was important to me. It became a competition. I didn't want to lose in the classroom or on the sports field. I finished high school with a 3.5 grade-point average and am proud to say I made Dean's List in college and earned my degree in Communications.

My favorite classes were math and biology. My all-time favorite class was in college—Hip Hop in Our Culture. I even wrote a rap song for extra credit. I love all sorts of music and my tastes are always changing. About the only music I don't like is heavy metal. When I'm with friends, I'd rather talk music or movies than basketball.

That's because basketball is part of my life but not who I am. You might be surprised to know I'm not a gym rat. I don't spend the whole day in the gym. I do

> When I'm in the gym, I work hard on my game.

> Jen and I at graduation.

FUN FACT >>> SUE'S VERY FIRST JOB WAS SELLING ICE CREAM NEAR A RACETRACK IN SARATOGA, CLOSE TO THE FAMILY'S SUMMER HOME. SHE WHEELED AROUND CARTS OF ICE CREAM. SHE RECEIVED LOW PAY AND DRY-ICE BURNS ON HER ARMS.

my workouts, practice hard for several hours, and then do other things. Life's too short to spend it all in a gym. Like most kids, I started playing basketball by shooting baskets with my sister and dad. We had a sorry hoop in our driveway. A city park wasn't far away, however, and that was the court of choice. I used to be picked last when park teams were formed. Later on, however, kids picked me first.

My earliest school basketball story was in kindergarten. My teacher asked if my dad played basketball. Yes, he did, I said. Which was true, he played hoops with me. The teacher assumed my father was Larry Bird and the rumor started, and has never really stopped.

AT LEAST A FEW TIMES EACH WEEK SOMEONE ASKS ME IF I'M RELATED TO FORMER BOSTON CELTIC GREAT LARRY BIRD. THE ANSWER IS NO! AT ONE POINT, I GOT SO SICK OF ANSWERING THE QUESTION I STARTED SAYING HE WAS MY UNCLE.

> Mom and I on the night of my eighth-grade graduation. I stayed out too long in the sun that day and got fried.

> My high school soccer teammates celebrate my 15th birthday.

Brad and I played like siblings. He became the brother I never had. We had many fierce one-on-one basketball games throughout the years. Brad and I are the same height, and we were evenly matched. Once we were in a gym playing and it got a little rough. I had just scored and was at the top of the key checking the ball. My throw wasn't directly at him and went off into a corner. I argued that he should go get it because he could have caught it. He argued that he wasn't the one who threw it and therefore shouldn't get it.

"You get it," I demanded.

"You threw it," he shot back.

NEITHER OF US MOVED FOR A HALF HOUR. WE WERE BOTH SO COMPETITIVE AND STUBBORN WE DIDN'T WANT TO GIVE IN. "YOU'RE SUCH A BABY," I SAID AS I FINALLY PICKED UP THE BALL.

I am ashamed to say I have been a baby about sports sometimes, too. My worst display of unsportsmanlike conduct happened at a youth track meet.

Dad was my track coach at the time and he placed me in the final of four legs of a relay. In this race our team was clearly the slowest. By the time my teammate passed the baton to me, all the other teams were far ahead. Instead of running, I stopped and threw the baton down and stomped off the track in a huff. There are times when you shouldn't be yourself, especially when you are feeling like a brat.

› I take the baton and run in the Penn Relays.

› Dad, Jen and I open gifts.

> My middle school team didn't have a No. 10 jersey so I doubled my favorite number and wore No. 20.

Despite that outburst, I consider myself a great teammate. That's very important to me. I have a good sense of balance on a team. There are some people who need to be pushed and others who need to be hugged. I've been skilled at telling the difference.

For me, I'd rather give an assist than score. I don't worry about scoring points. I only care about winning as a team. "Being yourself" is also about being there for other people. I generally shoot as needed. If our team is having trouble scoring, I'll shoot more. If we're winning, I'm happy to be the playmaker.

When I played AAU basketball, one of my coaches got so upset that I passed the ball so much he had a team meeting about it. He gave me a warning in front of the team. He said if I didn't shoot more he would take me out of games and sit me on the bench. Given that choice, I started shooting more for that coach.

One track coach bothered me so much I set a county record. I ran track in the spring during high school. Thanks to my speed and agility, the 400 hurdles was my best event. I set records wearing tennis shoes instead of track shoes with spikes.

Just before a race, a coach from another school saw me getting ready to run. He asked why I wasn't wearing spikes. "Do you know it will cost you .04 seconds? You should wear spikes!" he insisted.

I was stunned, to tell you the truth. I felt disrespected and put down. So I went out and showed him. I ran a personal best time of 1:05.

FUN FACT >>> FAVORITE MEAL: GRILLED CHEESE AND FRENCH FRIES. SUE ORDERED IT EVERY TIME SHE WENT INTO A LOCAL DINER FOR YEARS SO SHE COULD SAY, "HEY, FLO, GIVE ME THE USUAL."

23

> **Whether I went out on a date or just hung out with my high school friends, I enjoyed being around people.**

My parents respected me and trusted I would make good decisions when I was old enough to hang out with my friends on weekend nights. They never gave me a curfew. They did have one rule: I had to call home at II p.m. and tell them where I was, who I was with, and what time I'd be home.

The plan worked almost perfectly. I never abused their trust and was dependable. One night, however, Mom didn't hear from me at II p.m. My story is that I tried but didn't connect. By midnight Mom was in full panic. She called all over our town trying to find me. Parents were driving around looking for a friend and me. We were finally spotted by my friend's dad. We were just driving around. That's probably the one time my parents were very disappointed in me.

I upset some of my best friends my junior year when I decided to transfer to a high school in Queens, New York. I wanted to play basketball at the highest level possible. Christ the King High is only 20 miles away from Syosset—but it is worlds away from what I knew.

Syosset is Main Street suburbia with mostly white upper-class kids. Christ the King is in the heart of Queens and has a blend of all different races, nationalities, and religions. It was a culture shock and yet a very interesting place. The school also had a top girls' basketball program, and still does.

THIS WAS A REAL SACRIFICE FOR MY PARENTS. WE DECIDED TO RENT A SMALL APARTMENT IN QUEENS. DAD STAYED WITH ME ONE WEEK, MOM THE NEXT.

FUN FACT >>> SUE LOVES DAVE MATTHEWS BAND CONCERTS. SHE MAKES IT AN ALL-DAY THING AND HANGS OUT WITH FRIENDS.

By far the toughest thing about the move was my guilt about feeling I was breaking up the family. About the time I decided to transfer, my parents sat me down and told me they were planning to get a divorce. I went through the whole "what did I do" thing. My changing high schools proved to accelerate their breakup. That took its toll on me.

Moving to a new school is stressful enough. It helped that I knew many of the girls on the basketball team because I played against them in AAU basketball. Moving away from childhood friends wasn't easy.

I missed Brad the most. So we made a deal. He drove out to visit me every Wednesday night and we watched the TV show "Dawson's Creek" together. If you're wondering, Brad and I never dated. We've always been just friends. I did go out with other guys, but never had a serious boyfriend in high school.

Integrating into Queens definitely shaped my personality for the better. It made me a more well-rounded person, and I doubled my number of friends.

Playing for a powerhouse program taught me how to win. There's an attitude great teams have. It's a winning mentality. You know you're going to find ways to win. We won two state titles while I was there as the starting point guard. We were voted national champions my senior year as we went 27-0.

> Scoring a layup for Christ the King—two of my 1,700 high school points, which averaged 18 a game.

> Brad Barnett and I hanging out. Turns out we both made it to pro basketball. Brad is a writer for "NBA Buzz" at NBA.com.

The titles helped us seniors gain recognition. Five of the seniors from our team received college scholarships. I had my choice of many and narrowed my schools down to three. I decided on the University of Connecticut Huskies—UConn for short.

The Huskies were starting a tradition of winning women's basketball games with one national title before I got there. So expectations were rising for the UConn women.

I earned the starting guard job my freshman year but didn't live up to my hype. In my second game I picked up a technical foul because of this little flaw I have. Sometimes frustration on the court gets the best of me and a curse word, or two, slips out.

We were playing UCLA and I made a mistake and cursed myself. The referee heard me and thought I directed it to her and "T'd me up." That was the only time I have ever received a technical foul. The incident made me aware that how I react to situations in games has an influence on the young girls who watch our games. When you interact with people, "being yourself" is realizing the effect you have on others. I'm still working on taming my tongue during competition.

AS THE SEASON PROGRESSED I SHOT JUST 20 PERCENT AND MADE MORE TURNOVERS THAN ASSISTS. A CONNECTICUT NEWSPAPER HAD A HEADLINE: "SUE BIRD'S NOT THE ANSWER." PEOPLE STARTED TO DOUBT ME.

Eight games into the season I injured my knee during practice. It was season-ending bad. I tore my ligaments and needed surgery. Until then, I never had any injuries in sports at all. It was a blindside blow to be out. I hurt my knee on Dec. 14th and had surgery on Dec. 30th.

The next six months were the toughest of my life. Not only were they painful, but having to sit on the sidelines and watch practices and games broke my heart. It did, however, prove to be the turning point of my career.

I spoke with my parents and Jen by phone a lot and they helped me through it. My other friends also called and gave me encouragement, but this was the first time that I was forced to deal with a situation entirely on my own.

A teammate had the same surgery and she was my role model. After the surgery she said, "Now it's up to you. They'll tell you what to do for rehab, but it's up to you what kind of attitude you have."

She was so right. I've always been a positive person, and I wasn't going to let a setback change me. I decided I didn't want to be miserable around others. I didn't want to feel sorry for myself. I figured this was my fate, and I'd make the best of it.

MY ATTITUDE WORRIED THE UCONN COACHING STAFF. THEY CALLED MY DAD AND SAID, "WE'RE WORRIED ABOUT SUE. SHE'S TAKING THIS INJURY TOO WELL!"

I studied the game like never before and my sideline seat opened my eyes. That season I learned 10 times more by sitting and watching than I would've learned playing.

In the classroom I earned a 2.8 grade-point average, which is a C+. I remember thinking I don't want to be an average student. I didn't want to make excuses. The rest of my years in college I earned at least a 3.0 (B) in class.

> Sitting on the bench in street clothes taught me much about the game.

> A husky is Connecticut's mascot, which is why I'm standing in front of this statue on the UConn campus.

> My sophomore year we aimed high and celebrated a national championship.

My sophomore year I had plenty of motivation. It was a great year. We lost only once, to Tennessee on a last-second shot during the regular season. We got revenge and beat Tennessee for the national title.

My junior year brought high expectations. All our key people were back. Everyone picked us No. I, and many predicted we'd go undefeated. We didn't. We lost two games in the regular season (to Notre Dame and Tennessee).

That year was a tough one for me on and off the court. Still, I'll remember that year as one of my greatest thrills when I hit a game-winning shot in the Big East Championship game.

We faced Notre Dame in the semifinals of the Final Four and led by I5 points at halftime. But the Irish came back and we lost. Those of us who were juniors saved the pictures of us crying after the loss and put them in our lockers for motivation. Memory can sometimes be your best motivation.

During that year one of our assistant coaches gave me a book to read. Turns out it was a Positively For Kids book on Gary Payton called *Confidence Counts*. I remember how reading that book helped me. For me personally, my junior season wasn't as successful as my sophomore year and the reason was my confidence. I wasn't playing with confidence, so reading about Gary and how he approaches the game of basketball helped a lot. I knew then that I couldn't dwell on mistakes. I had to forget about the bad things, turnovers and missed shots, and continue to try and play my game. Confidence is what sets athletes apart, and I knew I needed to get mine back.

> UConn coach Geno Auriemma and I exchange words during a game.

> Swin Cash, left, Tamika Williams, and I take a break on the bench.

That year also marked the end of my longest dating relationship. I met Brett at the end of my sophomore year. We went out for a year until he decided to transfer to a different school. Our relationship didn't survive as boyfriend and girlfriend. We are still friends, though. We still talk sometimes. Who knows what would've happened if he stayed?

For my senior year we drew on inspiration from the school's past. Back in 1995, the UConn girls were undefeated, 35-0. As seniors, we wanted to finish with perfection. We'd say "35-0" in practice. We truly aimed to improve each day, each game.

OUR PRACTICES WERE TOUGHER THAN GAMES. COACH GENO AURIEMMA MADE US PRACTICE AGAINST COLLEGE-AGE GUYS. SOMETIMES WE'D PLAY FIVE OF US AGAINST SEVEN BOYS. PLAYING AGAINST STRONGER, QUICKER PLAYERS MADE US BETTER.

During one of those intense practices, the guy I covered hit a game-winner. Coach asked if I contested the shot, meaning did I play good defense. I didn't say anything. Coach asked the player if I contested the shot. He said no. I blurted out, "He's going to say what you want him to say. He's going to agree with you."

Doesn't sound so bad now, but to do that in front of the team and stand up to Coach Auriemma crossed the line. Coach verbally admonished me in front of everyone. The next day we cooled off. I apologized to Coach in front of the team, and he apologized for losing his temper.

FUN FACT >>> SUE IS ONE OF TWO UCONN PLAYERS TO RECORD MORE THAN 1,000 POINTS, 500 ASSISTS, AND 200 STEALS. JENNIFER RIZZOTTI IS THE OTHER.

That was the first time I had ever done that—stood up to a coach in front of the team—and I'll never do it again. Sometimes frustration can get the best of you mentally and physically. As a basketball player it's a constant battle, but one great athletes overcome. I've gotten along with all of my coaches. My best advice for young athletes is to buy into your coach's vision, even if you don't agree with it. If a coach says this is the way to run a play, don't fight it. As an athlete you have to understand that the coach runs the show. When you are on a team you are giving up part of yourself for the team. If I fought with a coach every step of the way I wouldn't be in the WNBA.

I'm not saying be a pushover. You have to pick your spots. If you have a real concern, you can talk with a coach away from the team. Depending on the issue, there are times to respectfully stand up for your opinion. Knowing when to speak up and when to listen goes with being comfortable with yourself.

I learned so much from Coach Auriemma. He taught me the most about leadership and how a point guard has to know her players—from birthdays to which buttons to push in each player for peak performance.

Throughout my college days I roomed with three teammates, all my same age. We were different people, from different backgrounds, who bonded together into true friends. Two of us were from the suburbs, one came from the projects, and another had a single parent and lived with her aunt.

I can honestly say we were all colorblind.

I shared a room with Swin Cash, who also made it to the WNBA and won a title with the Detroit Shock in 2004. Swin was from the inner city of Pittsburgh. We talked about our backgrounds all the time and how they shaped us. We didn't judge each other's background.

We got along by being true to ourselves. I grew as a person knowing them, and, hopefully, they learned something from me.

THE TRUE TEST OF YOUR FRIENDS IS WHEN YOU CAN BE YOURSELF AROUND THEM. IF YOU HAVE TO BE SOMEONE ELSE AROUND PEOPLE TO FIT IN, THEY AREN'T FRIENDS.

> I'm honored to receive the Sportswoman of the Year Award at the 2002 Women's Sports Foundation dinner.

> My college roommates (left to right) Asjha Jones, Swin Cash, Tamika Williams, and I hold the Sears Trophy in honor of our 2002 National Championship.

> My parents stand by my side at UConn's Senior Night.

> I celebrate a 3-point field goal.

Mostly we had fun together. We competed against each other in practice and at home. The four of us were competitive about everything. We pushed and challenged each other on and off the court. We'd play board games and card games whenever we were on the road.

One competitive test came on Senior Night. That's when UConn recognizes the seniors and their parents at the start of the last home game. Nobody wanted to cry during introductions. That night signaled the nearing end of our time together. We fought the tears, but we all eventually lost to our emotions.

My senior season ended with me dribbling the ball as the clock ran out. I kissed the ball and threw it in the air at the buzzer. UConn won its third national title, beating Oklahoma to finish 39-0—a perfect season!

The emotions of such a moment can't be described. It's so sweet. You want it to last. You work so hard to realize a dream and then it's over. I walked out of the locker room and my life as a professional began.

THE SEATTLE STORM SELECTED ME AS THE NO. 1 OVERALL PICK IN THE WNBA DRAFT. BEING THE TOP PICK MEANT I HAD THE OPPOSITE PROBLEM FROM MY FRESHMAN YEAR. INSTEAD OF PROVING PEOPLE WRONG, NOW I HAD TO PROVE PEOPLE RIGHT. I ACCEPTED THE CHALLENGE.

My first season in the WNBA brought many special memories. My first game was against my home-state team, the New York Liberty. I felt good about my 18-point, 6-assist game.

The Storm had not made the playoffs in its first two years, so that was definitely our top goal. We fought with Portland down the stretch for the last playoff spot. We won six straight, including an exciting win over Portland, in which I scored a franchise-record 33 points.

Two decisive losses to the Los Angeles Sparks eliminated us quickly in the playoffs. Still, we felt we had made positive steps.

My second season in Seattle proved more frustrating. New enthusiasm brought by new head coach Anne Donovan wasn't enough to overcome injuries to key people. I injured my knee in our first game and it never felt right the entire season. I couldn't use my quickness and hardly practiced. I had to rethink how I played.

We started among the league leaders, but losing two players to injury put us in a five-game losing nosedive. We almost made a comeback. In two of our last five games I had opportunities to win games in the final minutes and blew it on missed shots. Those losses kept us out of the playoffs. I felt strange. I had been in the playoffs nine straight years dating back to high school.

The highlights of the season were playing in the Fifth Annual WNBA All-Star game in New York's Madison Square Garden and watching Lauren Jackson shine all season.

SUPERSTITIONS

I'm very superstitious, I'm sorry to say. It's the whole theory if you wear a pair of socks and do well in a game, it must be the socks. I know deep down it's not the socks, but I know I feel better with a routine.

I have a whole bunch of them. When our team has our hands in the huddle, mine have to be on top. I tie my shoes a certain way and tuck my laces in. I use two hair bands and both have to be the same color, and I always wear a ponytail when playing sports. I like to eat certain things before a game, like pasta and chicken. I take a nap before games too. I normally keep these superstitions a secret.

In regular life I have certain rituals, too. When I walk on a plane, I touch the outside of the plane as I enter the doorway. I do the same thing when I get off.

THE ALL-STAR GAME FELT LIKE A HOMECOMING FOR ME. SO MANY OF MY FRIENDS, EVEN FORMER TEAMMATES FROM MY SOCCER DAYS, CAME AND WATCHED AND ATTENDED A POST-GAME PARTY I HOSTED. IT HELPED OUR WEST TEAM BEAT THE EAST A FIFTH-STRAIGHT TIME. I CONTRIBUTED 11 POINTS IN A GAME THAT FELT MORE LIKE A CHAMPION-SHIP CONTEST THAN AN EXHIBITION.

Lauren earned the WNBA's Most Valuable Player honor for the 2003 season. She averaged a league-leading 21.2 points per game and her 9.3 rebounds per game ranked fourth. She is the best player in the world, and I love playing with her because she makes my job so much easier. When someone on my team succeeds I'm not afraid to acknowledge them. Being secure with yourself allows you to praise the success of others.

My scoring dipped from 14.4 points per game my first year to 12.4 in 2003, as I knew it would thanks to my knee setback. Scoring for a point guard is over-rated anyway. The two stats I care about most are assists and turnovers. I aim for a 2-to-1 assist-to-turnover ratio. My assists average went from 5.9 per game to 6.5. I'm also proud I managed to start all 34 games despite the throbbing pain in my knee.

In sports and life, you can only give what you've got.

One thing the WNBA has taught me is you have to get over failures. You want to take the negative stuff and turn it into a positive. I want to remember how badly I felt in the locker room knowing we missed the playoffs, but I don't want to remember mistakes I made.

> I give pointers to a young player at a clinic; sing in a NIKE TV commercial; and pose for a photo op with LeBron James, Lisa Leslie, Usher, and Carmelo Anthony at the 2004 Read to Achieve event during the All-Star Weekend.

PLAYING BASKETBALL HAS GIVEN ME THE OPPORTUNITY TO HELP OTHERS OFF THE COURT.

The most rewarding charity events I've done are when I work with kids, either speaking at schools or doing camps and clinics. I've worked at many youth camps and have spoken at dozens of schools since my college days.

When I was growing up there weren't any female athletes on TV. So now, when I see little girls wearing my jersey it gives me a great deal of excitement because I would have loved to be able to look up to a female athlete. So I take it seriously and try to be as kind and as generous as I can.

I coached an 8th grade girls team during the 2003 winter season. To watch them improve was amazing. It made me think I might like to coach in the future.

My job as a WNBA player has allowed me to meet a lot of celebs. I took Nick Carter, from the Backstreet Boys, to the ESPYs as my date. I've met Justin Timberlake (personal fave), a lot of NBA guys, Ashton Kutcher, Danny Masterson, P. Diddy, Paris Hilton, etc. It kind of comes with the territory.

I've also had opportunities to make TV commercials. The most memorable has got to be the American Express commercial, where I chest-bumped an elderly woman. It was cute, funny, fun to do, and I've received only good feedback. I've been in a few now thanks to the promotional campaign by the WNBA, AmEx, ESPN, and Nike.

The Nike commercial I was in was one of LeBron's. It's the one where a gym is like a church of basketball. There are a bunch of us WNBA players in it. We are choir singers in the background.

Generally, making commercials is easy because of the creative fun in the air, but the early mornings and the "hurry up and wait" schedule can be hard to deal with.

FUN FACT >>> SUE IS ONE OF FOUR ACTIVE PLAYERS ON THE ADVISORY COUNCIL FOR JR. NBA/JR. WNBA PROGRAMS. TO LEARN MORE, GO TO WWW.NBA.COM/JRNBA/

SUE BIRD
WNBA
ACCOMPLISHMENTS
2002-2003

- Only WNBA player to make All-WNBA first team and start in WNBA All-Star game in first two seasons in league

- Named First Team All-WNBA in 2003 and 2002

- Western Conference All-Star starter in 2003, scoring II points, and 2002, handing out record-tying seven assists

- Set a record during the 2003 season with seven point-assist double-doubles

- Became just the third player in WNBA history to record 200 assists during the 2003 season

- Scored career-high and then-franchise-record 33 points on 8/9/02 vs. Fire

- In WNBA debut, notched 18 points, six assists, three steals, and three rebounds on 5/30/02 vs. Liberty

COLLEGE HIGHLIGHTS

- Member of NCAA Division I Championship Connecticut in 2000 and 2002

- Two-time All-American

- 2002 Associated Press and Naismith Player of the Year

- Recipient of the first annual Senior CLASS Award, presented to the nation's most outstanding senior basketball player

- Three-time Conseco/Nancy Lieberman-Cline National Point Guard of the Year Award winner

NCAA WOMEN'S CHAMPIONS

1993 Texas Tech def. Ohio St., 84-82
1994 North Carolina def. Louisiana Tech, 60-59
1995 Connecticut def. Tennessee, 70-64
1996 Tennessee def. Georgia, 83-65
1997 Tennessee def. Old Dominion, 68-59
1998 Tennessee def. Louisiana Tech, 93-75
1999 Purdue def. Duke, 62-45
2000 Connecticut def. Tennessee, 71-52
2001 Notre Dame def. Purdue, 68-66
2002 Connecticut def. Oklahoma, 82-70
2003 Connecticut def. Tennessee, 73-68
*2004 Connecticut def. Tennessee, 70-61

*UConn becomes first NCAA Division I school to win men and women's basketball championships in the same year.

SUE BIRD'S STATS

UCONN

Year	GP	FGM-A	Pct	3FGM-A	Pct	FTM-A	Pct	Reb	Avg	A	TO	B	S	Pts	Avg
'98-99	8	16-41	.390	6-19	.316	3-4	.750	16	2.0	25	16	I	15	41	5.1
'99-00	37	140-279	.502	72-145	.497	53-59	.898	94	2.5	160	80	I	69	405	10.9
'00-01	34	137-309	.443	60-139	.432	35-45	.778	89	2.6	169	88	4	63	369	10.9
'01-02	39	198-392	.505	69-148	.466	98-104	.942	131	3.4	231	93	9	96	563	14.4

WNBA (SEATTLE STORM)

Year	GP	FGM-A	Pct	3FGM-A	Pct	FTM-A	Pct	Reb	Avg	A	TO	B	S	Pts	Avg
2002	32	151-375	.403	57-142	.401	102-112	.911	83	2.6	191	109	3	55	461	14.4
2003	34	155-368	.421	49-140	.350	61-69	.884	113	3.30	221	110	I	48	420	12.4

The most embarrassing moment of my first two years with the Storm happened off the court while I was a guest in a radio studio. Players are often asked to help promote the league and our team. I do what I can. I speak at schools and community events. I sign autographs after the games. I do newspaper, radio, and TV interviews. So going on a radio talk show is a natural thing for me and part of my job.

During an interview in Seattle, the sports radio host proposed a friendly bet. It seemed harmless and good-natured at the time. It dealt with my assist-to-turnovers numbers at the end of the season. The provocative talk-show personality said if I lost the bet then I would have to let him "spank" me. Without thinking, I agreed to his challenge.

About a month later, a sportswriter wrote a story about it, including comments from a Washington state senator who blasted me for being insensitive to women who have suffered violence. The story spread and other newspapers and media across the country made a big deal about it. The stories twisted the impression people had of me. I was viewed in a light that wasn't me.

When the story broke, I immediately made a public statement. First, I apologized for offending anyone. Then I said the bet is off, and I took responsibility. I didn't blame the radio host for tricking me. I said I should have known better than to make such a bet.

GIRL TALK

You should resist your coach if he or she demands you do something unethical or touches you improperly. Then you need to tell your parents and teachers about it. Nothing like that has ever happened to me, but it does happen, unfortunately.

POWER OF SPEECH

Looking back on the radio incident, I didn't realize the power of such an event. Everyone who knows me understands I would never joke about such things. I've never had to deal with abuse and violence against women, so it was a learning experience. I was shocked and saddened to learn four women die each day of domestic violence in America. Between 2 and 4 million women (nobody really knows the exact number) are victims of violence each year in the United States. If you are confronted with violence or know someone who has been, there are organizations that can help you and your family.

Hotline for women of violence:

National Domestic Violence Hotline
1.800.799. SAFE (7233)
www.ndvh.org

> 2004 USA team members Diana Taurasi, Sheryl Swoopes, and I share a laugh during introductions at an exhibition game.

After my second season with the Storm, I had successful knee surgery to fix my problem, and after rehab the knee felt great.

I SIGNED A MULTIYEAR CONTRACT EXTENSION WITH THE STORM AND WAS HONORED TO BE CHOSEN TO PLAY ON THE 2004 U.S.A. OLYMPIC WOMEN'S BASKETBALL TEAM.

Playing in the Olympics will be amazing, especially in Athens, Greece, the birthplace of the Games. We have a great team and I look forward to helping any way I can.

There's been a lot of talk about the risk of terrorism at the Games. To tell you the truth, I try not to think about it. I'll take precautions. But it's hard to live in fear, so I don't let fear into my thinking. If you do, pretty soon you're afraid to cross the street. I can't live that way.

I look forward to the future with confidence, yet realize I must continue to work on improving each day, on and off the court. Being yourself is not an excuse for apathy, laziness, or failure. You either improve your game or you lose it. Ultimately, competition isn't about defeating others, it's about testing yourself.

If you take anything away from this book, I hope you'll believe that being yourself is good enough. I also hope you'll push yourself to find out how good you can be. I believe everyone has at least one great talent. If you love sports, go for it. If sports isn't for you, that's fine. Find what is for you.

Whatever your talents, there is only one you and that makes you valuable to this world, to your community, to your team, to your family. At times you might feel alone and left out, but there is a team for you—a group of people who will appreciate what you have to offer. You have a role in this world. So be yourself and have the courage to discover your best self.

> Senda Berenson   > The All-American Red Heads

> Seattle Storm coach
Anne Donovan, left, in 1979

THREE THINGS YOU SHOULD KNOW ABOUT WOMEN'S BASKETBALL

1. THE MOTHER

Senda Berenson is considered the mother of women's basketball. Berenson, a physical education director at Smith College in Boston, read about the new sport James Naismith invented in late 1891. Intrigued, she visited Naismith to learn more. Following that meeting, she rewrote basketball rules to fit the perceived physical limitations of women at the time.

She organized the first women's collegiate basketball game on March 21, 1893. Her women's rules were published in 1899. Among her rule changes:

- Women's teams had six players instead of five.
- The women's court was divided into three areas, and two players from each team had to stay in an assigned area.
- Attempting to steal the ball wasn't allowed.
- Dribbling was limited to three bounces.
- A player could only hold the ball for three seconds.

Berenson and Delta State coach Margaret Wade were the first two women elected into the Basketball Hall of Fame.

2. WOMEN'S PROFESSIONAL BASKETBALL

The first women's basketball team to pay its players was the All-American Red Heads. The barnstorming team was formed in 1936 and played for 50 years. The women dyed their hair red and put on exhibition games against men that amused and entertained. Hazel Walker, who played for the Red Heads, formed her own team in 1949 called the Arkansas Travelers. They played competitive games against men and won 85 percent of their games over 16 years.

The first attempt at a women's league came in 1975 with the Women's Professional Basketball Association. It disbanded before the season started. The Women's Basketball League had a three-season run from 1978–81. It started with eight teams but finished with just two. Team names included the Dallas Diamonds, California Dreams, Milwaukee Does, Minnesota Fillies, and Iowa Cornets.

Eight women's leagues have come and gone in three decades—two in the 1970s, three in the '80s and three in the '90s. The Women's National Basketball Association has been the most successful. It began in 1997 with eight teams playing 28 games. The WNBA partners with the National Basketball Association and plays in NBA venues during the summer. In 2004, 13 teams played a 34-game schedule. The salaries range from a minimum of $30,000 to $85,000, depending on years of service. Star players' pay may exceed the maximums.

A "minor league" women's professional league started in 2001. The National Women's Basketball League plays from January to April and in 2004 had six teams.

3. TITLE IX

No law has meant more to women in sports than Title IX.

Title IX of the Education Amendments of 1972 prohibits discrimination on the basis of sex in educational programs and activities at educational institutions that receive federal funds. It is an education law affecting all curricular and extra curricular offerings, from medicine, law and science to drama, dance and athletics.

Source: Women's Sports Foundation

Before Title IX:

- Many schools and universities had separate entrances for male and female students.

- Female students were not allowed to take certain courses, such as auto mechanics or criminal justice; male students could not take home economics.

- Most medical and law schools limited the number of women admitted to 15 or fewer per school.

- Many colleges and universities required women to have higher test scores and better grades than male applicants to gain admission.

- After winning two gold medals in the 1964 Olympics, swimmer Donna de Varona could not obtain a college swimming scholarship. For women they did not exist.

Source: Report Card on Gender Equity, National Coalition for Women and Girls in Education, 1997

After Title IX:

- In 1973, 43 percent of female high school graduates were enrolled in college. This grew to 63 percent in 2001.

- In 1971, 18 percent of young women and 26 percent of young men had completed four years or more of college; in 1994, 27 percent of both men and women had earned bachelor's degrees.

- In 1972, women received 9 percent of medical degrees, but by 2001 that number had moved up to 43 percent; 1 percent of dental degrees grew to 38 percent in 2001; and the percentage of law degrees earned by women had moved from 7 percent in 1971 to 47 percent in 2001.

- The number of girls playing high school sports has risen from 294,000 in 1971 to 2.8 million in 2003. Women playing college sports increased fivefold during that same time.

- 80 percent of female managers of Fortune 500 companies have a sports background.

- High school girls who participate in team sports are less likely to drop out of school, smoke, drink, or become pregnant.

Source: Title IX: 25 Years of Progress, U.S. Department of Education, 1997

National Center for Education Statistics

WOMEN'S PROFESSIONAL BASKETBALL LEAGUES

1936	All-American Red Heads	Exhibition games	50 seasons
1949	Hazel Walker's Arkansas Travelers	Exhibition games	16 seasons
1975	Women's Professional Basketball Association	6 teams	Disbanded before season
1978-81	Women's Basketball League	8 teams	3 seasons
1980-81	Ladies Professional Basketball Association	6 teams	Disbanded after 5 games
1984	Women's American Basketball Association	6 teams	1 season
1986	National Women's Basketball Association	8 teams	Disbanded before season
1991	Liberty Basketball Association	6 teams	Disbanded after 1 game
1993-95	Women's Basketball Association	12 teams	3 seasons
1996-98	American Basketball League	9 teams	2 complete seasons
1997-present	Women's National Basketball Association	13 teams	'04 marked 8th season
2001-present	National Women's Basketball League	6 teams	'04 marked 4th season